Pebble® Plus

MILITARY BRANCHES

THE U.S. ARMY

by Matt Doeden

Consulting Editor: Gail Saunders-Smith, PhD

Consultant: John Grady
Director of Communications, Association of the United States Army

Capstone press®

Mankato, Minnesota

Pebble Plus is published by Capstone Press,
151 Good Counsel Drive, P.O. Box 669, Mankato, Minnesota 56002.
www.capstonepress.com

1 2 3 4 5 6 13 12 11 10 09 08

Library of Congress Cataloging-in-Publication Data
Doeden, Matt.
   The U.S. Army / by Matt Doeden.
     p. cm. — (Pebble plus. Military branches)
     Includes bibliographical references and index.
     ISBN-13: 978-1-4296-1733-8 (hardcover)
     ISBN-10: 1-4296-1733-0 (hardcover)
     1. United States. Army — Juvenile literature. I. Title. II. Series.
UA25.D64 2009
355.00973 — dc22
                                          2008001752

Summary: Simple text and photographs describe the U.S. Army's purpose, jobs, tools, and machines.

Editorial Credits
Gillia Olson, editor; Renée T. Doyle, designer; Jo Miller, photo researcher

Photo Credits
DVIC/PH3 Shawn Hussong, 17; SGT Brandon Aird, 7; Sgt 1st Class Robert C. Brogan, 21; SGT Igor Paustovski,
    18; SPC Joshua Balog, 13; SRA Priscilla Robinson, 9; SSGT Eric T. Sheler, 5; SSGT Shane A. Cuomo, 15
Getty Images Inc./AFP/Mauricio Lima, 11
Shutterstock/EchoArt, 3
U.S. Army photo, 1
U.S. Army photo by Staff Sgt Russell L. Klika, front and back cover, 22

Artistic Effects
iStockphoto/Piotr Przeszlo (metal), cover, 1
Shutterstock/Tamer Yazici (camouflage), cover, 1, 24

Note to Parents and Teachers

The Military Branches set supports national science standards related to science,
technology, and society. This book describes and illustrates the U.S. Army. The images
support early readers in understanding the text. The repetition of words and phrases
helps early readers learn new words. This book also introduces early readers to
subject-specific vocabulary words, which are defined in the Glossary section. Early
readers may need assistance to read some words and to use the Table of Contents,
Glossary, Read More, Internet Sites, and Index sections of the book.

Table of Contents

What Is the Army?

The Army is a branch of the
United States Armed Forces.
People in the Army
keep the country safe.

Army Jobs

People in the Army
are called soldiers.
Infantry soldiers fight
battles on the ground.

Army pilots fly helicopters.

Pilots use Black Hawk

helicopters to carry

soldiers and supplies.

Army mechanics fix machines.

The Army has
many other jobs.
Some soldiers are doctors,
cooks, or police officers.

13

Tools and Machines

The Army uses tanks.

The M1 Abrams is

its main tank.

Soldiers ride in Humvees.
These trucks have armor
to keep soldiers safe.

The Army uses weapons.

Soldiers carry M-16 rifles.

Grenades and missiles

blow up enemy targets.

Keeping Us Safe

The brave soldiers

of the Army

fight for our country.

They risk their lives

to keep us safe.

Glossary

Armed Forces — the whole military; the U.S. Armed Forces include the Army, Navy, Air Force, Marine Corps, and Coast Guard.

armor — a strong covering used to keep things or people safe

branch — a part of a larger group

grenade — a small weapon used to blow up a target; grenades are thrown by a person or fired by a gun.

mechanic — a soldier who fixes Army planes, tanks, trucks, and other machines

missile — a large weapon used to blow up a target

rifle — a weapon that can fire bullets very fast

tank — an armored vehicle that moves on two tracks

target — an object at which to aim or shoot

Read More

Doeden, Matt. *The U.S. Army.* The U.S. Armed Forces. Mankato, Minn.: Capstone Press, 2005.

Ellis, Catherine. *Helicopters.* Mega Military Machines. New York: PowerKids Press, 2007.

Zuehlke, Jeffrey. *Tanks.* Pull Ahead Books. Minneapolis: Lerner, 2006.

Internet Sites

FactHound offers a safe, fun way to find Internet sites related to this book. All of the sites on FactHound have been researched by our staff.

Here's how:

1. Visit *www.facthound.com*

2. Choose your grade level.

3. Type in this book ID **1429617330** for age-appropriate sites. You may also browse subjects by clicking on letters, or by clicking on pictures and words.

4. Click on the **Fetch It** button.

FactHound will fetch the best sites for you!

Index

Word Count: 121
Grade: 1
Early-Intervention Level: 23